— How to —
DRINK COFFEE

For Peter and Peter

First published in the United Kingdom in 2023
by Skittledog, an imprint of Thames & Hudson Ltd,
181A High Holborn, London WC1V 7QX

British Library Cataloguing-in-Publication Data
A catalogue record for this book is available from
the British Library

ISBN 978-1-837-76022-0

Printed and bound in China by C&C Printing Offset Co., Ltd

Senior Editor: Jodi Simpson
Designer: Masumi Briozzo
Production: Felicity Awdry

Be the first to know about our new releases,
exclusive content and author events by visiting
skittledog.com
thamesandhudson.com
thamesandhudsonusa.com
thamesandhudson.com.au

— How to — DRINK COFFEE

SARAH FORD

Skittledog

Contents

A Rich History

It is hard to imagine all that goes into producing your morning coffee. The humble coffee bean has been travelling around the world for hundreds of years, and there is a rich history of stories about how beans have been exported, traded, smuggled and stolen. Coffee was supposedly discovered in Ethiopia in 700 CE. It is said that a goat herder noticed his goats were dancing around strangely after eating red berries that they had found on the ground. He sampled the fruit from the nearby evergreen bushes for himself and felt ecstatic. Rumour has it that the herder shared his findings with a monk, who ate the fruits to help him stay up at night and pray.

There is little doubt that the stimulation provided by coffee has a big part to play in its enduring popularity. In fact, the coffeehouse came into being in the Ottoman Empire, where coffee was considered to be the best alternative to alcohol, which was banned. The coffeehouse was also a place to gather, talk, share ideas and socialise. Political sentiments often developed there, which lead to coffeehouses being banned when political rule was challenged. Coffeehouses were found in Vienna, Damascus and Constantinople by the 1500s. At this time, coffee was often sweetened to make it more palatable. By the 17th century, coffee, tea and chocolate were all popular in England, where the first coffeehouse had opened in 1652. Demand grew, with many more opening and playing a part in English society.

Coffee has come a long way since then. Today, the taste is exceptional, with many growers, producers and varieties to choose from. All the processes that go into producing the drink we know and love have been finely honed, and growers produce specialty varieties and blends all around the world. However you drink it, one thing remains constant: the delight that a good cup of coffee can bring. But it's not just for drinking – coffee can take cakes, cookies and even savoury food to new levels of deliciousness.

From Bush to Bean to Cup

The coffee beans we know and love are the seeds of a coffee cherry, so called because they are a bright red when they are ripe and ready to be picked. The cherries grow on a bush or tree, which can take three to four years to start producing fruit. The fruit is harvested once or twice a year, usually by hand, and needs to be processed quickly.

First, the seeds – which become the coffee beans – are removed from the pulp of the fruit and placed in water tanks to ferment for up to 36 hours. After this, they are washed to remove any remaining pulp and then spread out to dry in the sun. A more traditional method involves drying the whole cherries in the sun, periodically raking and turning them over, and covering them at night; it can take several weeks for all the moisture to dry out. The beans must then be hulled to remove the outer layers of the fruit. They are then sorted by size and weight and any defective beans are removed. These beans, called 'green coffee', are exported in jute bags by ship.

Taste and roasting

Coffee is tasted many times in a process known as cupping. The beans are looked at to check their quality, then they are roasted in a laboratory, ground up and infused with boiling water. The aroma of the coffee is 'nosed', a spoonful is slurped with a view to covering all the taste buds and the tongue, then the coffee is spat out. The tasters describe the sweetness, acidity, balance and flavour of the coffee.

The roasting process changes the green coffee into the brown beans that we buy. The beans are roasted in machines set to 288°C and are kept moving to avoid burning. When they turn brown, they release an aromatic oil.

Recipe Notes

This book includes recipes made with nuts and nut derivatives. Anyone who has allergic reactions to nut or nut derivatives, or who is vulnerable to allergies, is advised to avoid dishes made with them.

Standard level spoon measurements are used:
1 tablespoon = 15ml
1 dessertspoon = 10ml
1 teaspoon = 5ml

Espresso: 1 shot = 7g ground coffee/30ml espresso.

Alcohol: 1 measure = 25ml.

Ovens should be preheated to the specified temperature. For fan ovens, follow the manufacturer's instructions to adjust the time and temperature.

Coffee Origin and Taste

The Americas
The majority of the world's coffee is supplied by the Americas. From Brazil to Guatemala, there is a wide range of beans, often characterised as smooth and sweet, well balanced with a bright acidity and a crisp and clean taste. The aroma of these coffees is often described as pure, with notes of chocolate, nuts, fruits and spices. Some of the most expensive coffees come from Central America. One of the reasons that these coffees are so popular is that they are consistently balanced. There is great variety and quality.

The Caribbean
Caribbean beans are known for their balance and mildly acidic flavour. They are uncomplicated, rich and smooth with notes of wine and smoke. The coffees are soft and almost creamy but tend to lack intense top notes. While clean and pleasant to drink, they are not particularly complex.

Asia
Asian coffees are not as popular as their counterparts in Africa and South America. That said, there are some that think Pacific coffee has a lot to offer. Asian coffees vary, but they tend to be full bodied with earthy, woody notes. They have a mild acidity but can be slightly bitter with a salty aftertaste. Coffees from South-East Asia tend to be either loved or hated.

Africa
Ethiopia is the birthplace of coffee, and Africa is thought to have some of the best beans in the world. Central and Eastern Africa grow and export large amounts of coffee. Each country has different techniques, making its coffees unique. African coffee is often known for its floral, fruity and berry notes and complex flavours. The acidity is bright, and there are hints of citrus and jasmine florals. African coffee is very diverse, with many varieties grown across the continent.

Know Your Beans

There are four main types of coffee bean: Arabica, Robusta, Liberica and Excelsa. They each have their own unique taste profile.

Arabica

This is the best-known and most popular coffee bean, the most commonly produced and the best quality. Arabica beans are grown at high altitudes and need shade and steady rain. The plants are easy to look after, aromatic and flavoursome – hence their popularity.

Robusta

The second most produced, Robusta beans are resilient and hardy, and therefore easy to produce. The beans are grown in hot climates and need less rain than Arabica. They are high in caffeine but have a sharper flavour, often described as chocolatey.

Liberica

Liberica beans are less common, irregular in shape and larger. They grow on tall trees and are harvested by pickers on ladders. The flavour of the beans is described as smoky, floral and fruity with a unique aroma.

Excelsa

These beans have recently been reclassified as members of the Liberica family, but they taste very different. The small, round beans have complex flavours of berries with chocolate notes.

Know Your Coffee

Ristretto

Espresso

Lungo
espresso

Macchiato

Cortado

Cappuccino

Latte

Flat white

Mocha

Americano

Affogato

Steamy

If there is a better way to start your day
than with coffee, I don't know what it is.
Whether you take your coffee short and
dark or long and creamy, the aroma will
lift your senses, the mug will warm your
hands and the taste will enliven your
body. Coffee can kick-start a good day
or make a bad one more bearable.

How to Choose the Right Milk

Milk can make all the difference to a cup of coffee. There are many different kinds of milk available and different ways to use them, depending on what kind of coffee you're preparing.

What is the best milk to use?

The milk you use is entirely up to you and your personal taste, but some types of milk naturally lend themselves better to coffee than others. Cappuccinos and lattes are best made with full-fat or whole milk, as they contain protein and fat that helps with the flavour and foam. A coffee made with skimmed milk has a more intense flavour but one that won't last as long. Oat milk is considered to be the best non-dairy alternative, especially the barista editions, as it is flavoursome and it froths and steams well. Soy milk is best avoided as it is difficult to froth and has a tendency to curdle.

Air and heat

To turn your everyday chilled milk into something silky, velvety and creamy, you simply have to introduce air into it and heat it – this is called stretching the milk. It can be done easily at home and the milk can then be used in different ways to transform your coffee: scoop it on top of a cappuccino or whip it into a latte.

Froth or steam?

Steamed milk is hot milk that produces a delicate foam. Adding steam aerates and heats the milk. This is often done with a steaming wand, though it can be done successfully at home without a wand (see page 18). It makes the milk hot and frothy by breaking down the fat into tiny air bubbles known as microfoam. Steamed milk has a heavier, smoother texture than frothed milk and can be used in many coffee drinks.

Frothed milk is made by aerating the milk to add air bubbles and create a frothy, lighter texture (see page 19). The technique produces larger bubbles that hold their shape to create foam. Frothed milk tends to be used in foam-filled beverages such as cappuccinos. It should be airy to drink and can be used hot or cold.

Mastering the Perfect Pour

With your steamed milk (see page 18) in a jug, tap the jug on a work surface and give the milk a swirl to remove large air bubbles. The milk should have a velvety sheen and texture. The pouring technique is important: aim to pour the milk directly into the middle of the cup, then in a circular motion out to the edge of the cup. Hold back the foam with a spoon and then spoon the foam onto the top of your drink. Different drinks will need different amounts of milk and foam (see page 26).

How to Steam Milk

If you like your coffee with steamed milk, there are a few different ways you can prepare it. The perfect milk temperature is 65°C. For best results, use a food thermometer to check the temperature of the milk as you're heating it so you can stop the process at the perfect time and avoid scalding.

In the microwave

Fill ⅓ of a mug with the milk of your choice and heat in the microwave for about 30 seconds. You may have to experiment to determine the exact amount of time needed. If need be, microwave for a further 10 seconds, or until you have the right temperature.

On the hob

If you heat the milk in a pan on the hob, you will have more control over the heat. Milk can scald easily, so warm it over a low to medium heat, stirring regularly. This can take 1–3 minutes.

Using the frothing wand on an espresso machine

Fill a metal jug to the bottom of the wand's spout with your chilled milk of choice. Make sure the steam wand is clean and at the correct temperature. Place the wand just under the surface of the milk. This heats the milk and creates a small whirlpool. After 5-10 seconds, immerse the wand further. Keep steaming until the temperature reaches 65°C – the jug should be almost too hot to touch.

How to Froth Milk

Immersion
blender

Hob-top
frother

Handheld
electric frother

French press
frother

No-Frills Frothing

Pour your chosen chilled milk into a large
microwaveable jar or bottle with a sealed lid, so
that it is ⅓ full (or contains your desired amount).
Shake the milk vigorously until it doubles in size
and is frothy – this can take up to 1 minute. Remove
the lid and microwave the milk for 30 seconds.
This will set the foam. You will need to watch to
make sure that the milk doesn't overflow. If this
happens, pause the process to allow the milk to
settle, then start again. If the milk is not hot enough,
microwave for a further 10 seconds or until you
reach the desired heat.

How to Brew Coffee

Great coffee starts with the right equipment and the right beans.

Grinder

Coffee tastes best when it is freshly ground. If you grind beans as you need them, you will ensure you get the best flavour. An electric grinder is by far the easiest and most efficient way to grind beans, although you can also grind by hand. Coffee can be very fine, fine, medium or coarse ground according to how you intend to make your coffee (see page 21).

Scale

For weighing beans and grounds.

Kettle

A normal kettle is fine, but if you want to move to the next level you could invest in a pour-over kettle with a thermometer.

Filter papers

When buying filter papers check that you buy the right ones for the equipment you have. Each manufacturer will recommend a paper for their product. These are generally used for pour-over coffees.

Coffee beans

It is important to take your time to find the right coffee for you. Do you like the chocolatey tones of Brazilian coffee or the vibrant citrus flavours of Kenyan coffee? The best way to find out is to try different types, read reviews, attend tasting sessions and experiment in coffee shops. There are also many experts to be found in independent coffee shops and they will be pleased to share their knowledge.

The right grind

To get the best coffee, it is important to have the right grind for your brew method.

• Turkish – extra fine
• Espresso – fine
• Aeropress – medium fine
• Pour over – medium
• Home espresso machine – medium coarse
• French press – coarse
• Cold brew – extra coarse

The right water temperature

Your water should be 88-92°C, or just below boiling temperature. If you boil the kettle, let it cool a little before pouring.

Making Coffee in a Cafetière or French Press

• 18g coffee (1 rounded tablespoon); 300ml water = coffee for 1
• 30g coffee (2 rounded tablespoons); 500ml water = coffee for 2
• 60g coffee (4 rounded tablespoons); 1 litre water = coffee for 4

Brewing Methods

Everyone has their favourite coffee-brewing method. Here are the more common ones.

Cafetière or French press

This is a simple and quick way to make as many cups as you want by steeping medium-coarse ground coffee. Add the right amount of coffee for the number of cups you want to brew (see page 21), pour in the hot water (88–92°C) and allow it to steep for 3–4 minutes, then press down and serve.

Moka pot

A traditional stove-top brewing method from Italy that moves boiling water through coffee grounds in cycles. To use the pot, fill the bottom chamber to just below the valve with water preheated to around 70°C. Fill the filter with medium ground coffee – level it off but don't pack it down. Screw the top and bottom chambers together and place the pot on the hob over a high heat. When you hear the coffee bubbling, turn the heat off. Any residual heat will push enough water through to brew all the rest of the coffee. The process can take up to 10 minutes.

Pour over

This method brews the coffee straight into your mug through a filter paper. Place the pour-over brewer on top of your mug and add the filter. Add 15g of medium ground coffee to the filter paper and pour 300ml of boiled and slightly cooled water over the top of the grounds and allow the brewed coffee to drip through into the mug.

Chemex

The Chemex operates in a similar way to a pour-over brewer, but brews the coffee into a carafe instead of a mug, allowing you to make more than one cup at a time. You will need a thicker filter and medium-coarse ground coffee.

Espresso machine

These machines can be expensive, but they are an investment and well worthwhile if you are a coffee lover – if you use your machine daily, it will soon become worth the outlay. Espresso machines work by pushing pressurised hot water through tightly packed grounds in a filter. They often come with a built-in milk steamer. The downside to the machines is the cleaning and descaling they require, but many consider the effort worth it for a great shot of espresso. Each machine comes with an individual set of operating instructions.

Aeropress

This is a handheld, portable, manual coffee maker for one person. It works similarly to a syringe, with a plunger inserted into an outer tube. Ground filter or espresso coffee and boiled water are added to the tube. Once the grounds have steeped, the plunger forces them through a filter to produce concentrated, espresso-style coffee. An aeropress can also be used for filter or cold-brew coffee.

How to Make Espresso Without a Machine

If you don't want an expensive, bulky espresso machine, a moka pot or French press could be perfect for you.

A moka pot works in the same way as an espresso machine by forcing steam and boiling water through ground coffee and produces coffee very similar to an espresso.

Use 15g of medium ground, espresso-roasted coffee and 170ml of water and follow the instructions on page 22.

You can also make espresso in a French press or cafetière. Finely grind 2 tablespoons of espresso-roasted beans and warm your press. Add the coffee and a cup of boiled and slightly cooled water. Allow the coffee to steep, then gently stir. Add the filter, allow the coffee to brew for about 3 minutes, then press down slowly and pour a double or two single espressos.

The brew ratio

This is the ratio of coffee to water. Each different coffee will have a different brew ratio. A good starting point for an espresso is a ratio of 1:2 – 1 part coffee to 2 parts water. The final weight of the coffee drink should be twice the weight of the ground coffee. This ratio can be altered if your preference is for a smaller, stronger espresso like those typically made in Italy.

Crema

Crema – the creamy brown foam on top of the coffee – is possibly the most important part of espresso. It is created when slightly cooled boiled water emulsifies the oil in coffee. Traditionally, espresso was only considered good if it had a decent topping of crema, though some people find that it makes the coffee too bitter and scrape it off before drinking.

Espresso explained

• **Espresso** – a small, dark, intense drink, 30ml, made with finely ground coffee in a brew ratio of 1:2, with a small head of crema on top. A double espresso is 60ml and is known as a doppio espresso.

• **Ristretto** – a smaller, stronger 'restricted' espresso, 22ml, made with finely ground coffee and less water than espresso.

• **Lungo** – a longer espresso, 60ml, made with two or three times the amount of water as traditional espresso and a coarse-ground, lighter-roast coffee.

Demitasse

An espresso cup is known as a *demitasse*, from the French meaning 'half cup'. Small but perfectly formed, it measures 60-90ml – a little cup that holds a great deal of flavour and punches well above its weight.

Coffees with an Espresso Base

Macchiato

A macchiato – from the Italian for 'stained' or 'marked' – is an espresso with a spot of milk added to it, just enough to slightly lighten or 'stain' the dark colour of the coffee. In coffee shops it is often served topped with a little foam.

Latte

The latte, a light and milky coffee topped with froth, was developed for customers who found espresso too bitter and wanted a longer, less intense drink. If you like a milky coffee, this is the one for you. It is made with a single shot of espresso mixed with steamed milk and topped with frothed milk. It has more milk and a milder flavour than a cappuccino.

Cappuccino

The cappuccino is a layered coffee consisting of a double shot of espresso with the same amount of steamed milk and topped with foam. There should be a 1:1 ratio of liquid to foam. Dating back to the 19th century, the drink was named after Capuchin friars, who wore robes of the same colour.

Flat white

Hailing from Australasia, the flat white has been adopted all over the world. It is a smaller version of the latte, with 2 shots of espresso and a stronger coffee to milk ratio of 1:2, with just a touch of foam. It has the perfect topping for coffee art (see page 28).

Cortado

A Spanish coffee, served in a glass. A 30ml shot of espresso is combined with 30ml of steamed milk, making a small coffee with good flavour and no foam.

Americano

After World War 2, American soldiers based in Italy found that the espresso they were served was too strong for them – they wanted their coffee to resemble the filter coffee they drank at home and requested extra water with their espresso to dilute the taste. This coffee became known as *caffè americano* – 'American coffee'. Nowadays it is known as café Americano or just Americano. To make this at home, add slightly cooled boiled water to a cup and pour a double shot of espresso over the top. If the coffee is still too bitter, try scraping the crema off the top. Serve with milk on the side, if you like.

Should You Sprinkle Chocolate on a Cappuccino?

The short answer to this is that you can make your cappuccino however you like - use oat milk, add syrup or sprinkle the top with chocolate or cinnamon. It really is down to personal taste, though cappuccino in its true, original form does not have chocolate on the top.

Latte Art

If you go to an independent coffee shop, you may find the barista has adorned the top of your coffee with a beautiful work of art. Latte art is like the icing on a cake – a final flourish that lifts your coffee and brings joy. It shows that the barista is a craftsperson and that they have taken care with the preparation of your drink. From hearts to tulips to smiley faces, latte art is no mean feat: it requires perfectly frothed milk, great timing, a steady hand and perfect positioning. Practise makes perfect, so start simple and build up to creating masterpieces in your coffee at home.

The heart

Steam your milk (see page 18) and make sure you have plenty of foam, then add it to a jug. Pour your espresso into a coffee cup, then tilt the cup towards the jug of steamed milk. Add the milk to the tilted cup, pouring slowly in circles until the cup is half full and trying to keep the crema on the surface of the drink; hold the foam back with a spoon. Slowly place the cup on a flat surface. Move the jug so that it is right above the surface of the coffee and keep pouring so that the foam forms a blob on the surface of the coffee. Remember, it is the jug and milk that are moving and not the cup. When the cup is almost full, pour the milk in a line through the middle of the blob to the other side to create a heart shape. Present to someone you love.

Gingerbread Latte Like Christmas in a glass!

MAKES 2 MUGS
OR GLASSES

– 1 tablespoon ginger syrup
  (see page 60)
– 3 shots espresso
– 300ml full-fat milk or
  oat milk
– whipped cream, to top
– crushed ginger biscuit and
  cinnamon, for sprinkling
  (optional)

While you are brewing your espresso, warm the milk in a small pan on the hob until simmering. Turn off the heat and whisk the milk until light and frothy. Add the espresso and syrup to a tall heatproof glass, then add your frothy milk and stir gently. Top with whipped cream, crushed biscuit and cinnamon.

Coffee Mocha Warming and sweet, this drink is perfect for winter.

MAKES 1 MUG

– 25g dark chocolate,
  chopped
– 2 teaspoons hot
  chocolate powder
– 2 shots espresso
– hot milk, to top up
– whipped cream and mini
  marshmallows, to decorate
  (optional)

Place the chocolate in a mug and melt it slowly in a microwave, then stir well. Add the hot chocolate powder and espresso to the melted chocolate and mix thoroughly. Top up with hot milk. Decorate with whipped cream and marshmallows, if you like.

Pumpkin-Spice Latte A coffee drink full of traditional autumn flavours.

MAKES 1 MUG
OR GLASS

- 2 shots espresso
- 300ml full-fat milk or
  oat milk
- 2 tablespoons pumpkin
  purée, homemade
  (see page 33) or tinned
- 2 heaped teaspoons
  brown sugar
- 1 teaspoon Pumpkin
  Spice (see below)
- dash of vanilla extract

While you are brewing the espresso, warm the milk in a small pan on the hob until simmering. Turn off the heat and whisk the milk until light and frothy. Add the purée, sugar, spice and vanilla to a long heatproof glass and stir. Then add the espresso, stir again and add the frothy milk. Stir gently but well to mix.

Pumpkin Spice Add to Pumpkin-Spice Lattes and other coffee drinks for a taste of autumn.

MAKES ENOUGH FOR
ABOUT 25 DRINKS

- 1½ tablespoons
  ground cinnamon
- 2 teaspoons
  ground ginger
- ½ teaspoon
  ground nutmeg
- ¼ teaspoon
  ground cloves

Mix all the spices together and store in a sealed jar.

Pumpkin Purée You can make your own purée quite easily if you can't get hold of the tinned variety. Heat the oven to 200°C (Gas 6). Cut a pumpkin in half and remove the seeds. Place the halves flat side down on a roasting tin and roast for 40–60 minutes, depending on size. Once cooled, scrape out the flesh and blitz in a food processor until smooth.

Top 5 Things to Dunk in Coffee

- **Biscotti** (see page 86) – Designed by the Italians with dunking in mind.
- **Shortbread** – It won't fall apart and will melt in your mouth, not your coffee.
- **Almond horns** – The perfect shape and strength for dunking.
- **Doughnuts** – They're not called Dunkin' Donuts for nothing.
- **Gingerbread men** – Head first, hold on tight to the feet!

INTERNATIONAL COFFEE TRADITIONS

North Scandinavian *kaffeost* is prepared by adding cubes of Finnish cheese, made from reindeer milk, to a cup and pouring hot black coffee over the top. It is rich, smoky and buttery, and best served with a spoon, as the cheese does not melt but rather absorbs the coffee.

Brazil's *cafezinho* is like an espresso but stronger. It is dense, black and very sweet, and a traditional part of local hospitality.

In **Turkey** it is customary to serve coffee with a glass of water. A sip of water is taken to clear the palate so it is ready to experience the full taste of the strong, sweet, black coffee. Coffee is served to the oldest person in the room first, as a sign of respect. It is accompanied by a sweet treat, such as Turkish delight.

Coffee in the **Middle East** is all about hospitality, with the first drink offered to a guest. Rich in flavour and with added spices, the coffee is served black, often with dried dates for sweetness.

In **Vietnam**, the locals like their coffee strong and bitter, but with the added sweetness of condensed milk. It is usually made in a French press and can be served hot or cold.

In **Malaysia**, the locals drink a blend of coffee and tea known as *yuanyang*, with a ratio of 3 parts black coffee to 7 parts milky tea. It is served hot or cold.

Irish Coffee The perfect end to dinner.

MAKES 1 TALL GLASS

– 150ml strong-
  brewed coffee
– 2 measures Irish whiskey
– 1 teaspoon brown sugar
– 1 measure double cream
– pinch of nutmeg,
  to decorate

Pour the coffee into a heatproof glass, add
the whiskey and sugar and gently stir to mix.
Gently pour the cream over the back of a spoon
onto the surface of the coffee so that it forms a
creamy layer. Decorate with a pinch of nutmeg.

Calypso Coffee This drink is similar to an
Irish coffee but has the taste of the Caribbean with
dark rum and sugar.

MAKES 1 TALL GLASS

– 150ml strong-
  brewed coffee
– 1 measure coffee liqueur
– 1 measure dark rum
– 1 teaspoon brown sugar
– 1 measure double cream

Pour the coffee into a heatproof glass, add the
liqueur, rum and sugar and gently stir to mix.
Gently pour the cream over the back of a spoon
onto the surface of the coffee so that it forms a
creamy layer.

French Coffee An orange kick makes this coffee sweet and delicious.

MAKES 1 TALL GLASS

- 150ml strong-brewed coffee
- 1 measure coffee liqueur
- 1 measure orange liqueur
- 1 teaspoon brown sugar
- whipped cream and grated chocolate, to decorate

Pour the coffee into a heatproof glass, add the liqueurs and sugar, and gently stir to mix. Top with whipped cream and the chocolate.

Hot White Russian This hot version of the classic cocktail is a great winter warmer.

MAKES 1 SHORT GLASS

- 1 measure vodka
- 1 measure coffee liqueur
- 1 shot espresso
- 2 measures steamed oat milk or cream, frothed, to top up

Pour the vodka and coffee liqueur into a short heatproof glass, add the espresso, then top up with the steamed milk or cream.

Mexican Coffee Chilli complements coffee, chocolate and cinnamon flavours.

- 25g dark chocolate, chopped
- 1 pinch cinnamon
- 1 pinch chilli powder
- 2 shots espresso
- 1 measure dark coffee liqueur
- 1 measure white tequila
- whipped cream and grated chocolate, to decorate (optional)

Gently melt the chocolate in a saucepan over a low heat. Add the spices and espresso to the melted chocolate and mix thoroughly. Take the saucepan off the heat and add the liqueur and tequila. Stir well and pour into a heatproof glass. Decorate with whipped cream and grated chocolate, if you like.

Chilled

Hot days are made for chilled coffees. Sit back and relax with one of these delicious recipes – simple but impressive to make for yourself or for guests. If you're having a party, the chilled cocktails are guaranteed to get things going.

Coffee Lassi

A sweet and creamy yogurt drink that is lovely with breakfast.

MAKES 2 GLASSES

- 250ml full-fat milk, chilled
- 4 tablespoons natural Greek yogurt
- 2 dessertspoons maple syrup
- 2 double shots espresso, cooled
- ice
- ½ teaspoon ground cardamom, plus extra for decorating

Blitz all the ingredients in a blender until well mixed. Serve over ice and decorate with a sprinkle of cardamom powder.

Nutty Banana and Coffee Milkshake

A delicious breakfast milkshake to start the day right.

MAKES 1 TALL GLASS OR 2 SMALL GLASSES

- 2 shots espresso, cooled
- 1 small banana, chopped
- 1 teaspoon vanilla extract
- 1 teaspoon clear honey
- 150ml oat milk
- 1 rounded dessertspoon peanut butter
- whipped cream and grated chocolate, to serve

Blitz all the ingredients in a blender until smooth and creamy. Serve over ice and top with whipped cream and grated chocolate.

Coffee and Date Smoothie The perfect
way to kick-start your day.

MAKES 1 TALL GLASS

– 1 small banana
– 2 pitted dates
– 1 dessertspoon
  porridge oats
– 1 rounded dessertspoon
  tahini
– 1 tablespoon
  natural yogurt
– ½ teaspoon vanilla extract
– 2 shots espresso, cooled
– 150ml oat milk
– ice

Blitz all the ingredients in a blender until
smooth. Serve over ice.

Mudslide
A rich, chocolatey, boozy milkshake, excellent as an after-dinner treat.

MAKES 1 GLASS

- 25g dark chocolate, melted
- 1 measure coffee liqueur
- 1 measure vodka
- 1 measure coffee cream liqueur
- 2 measures double cream
- ice

Place the melted chocolate in a saucer. Dip the rim of an old fashioned glass in to the melted chocolate, then allow the chocolate to drip down the glass. Place in the refrigerator for 10 minutes until hard. Add all the ingredients to a cocktail shaker with ice and shake well. Add some ice to the prepared glass, then strain the cocktail into it.

Wake the Dead
This cocktail is not for the faint hearted, but it will keep the party going! To make more than one drink, double or triple the ingredients accordingly.

MAKES 1

- ½ shot espresso, cooled
- 1 measure tequila
- 1 measure tequila-based coffee liqueur

Place all the ingredients in a cocktail shaker with ice and shake to mix. Strain into an old fashioned glass and serve ice cold.

How to Make Cold-Brew Coffee

Place 50g of ground coffee (your choice) into a large jug and add 400ml of cold water. Do not stir, just cover and allow to steep for 12–24 hours. Gently stir, then pour through a funnel lined with a paper coffee filter into another jug or large jar. Store in the refrigerator for up to two weeks.

Brew time: 12–24 hours

Brewing process: Brewed with cold or room-temperature water, never heated

Served: Diluted with water or milk, usually over ice

Flavour: Smooth, malty or chocolatey rather than bitter and acidic

Storage: 10–14 days in the refrigerator

How to Make Iced Coffee

Simply make a hot pot of coffee, sweeten to taste with sugar (optional) and leave it to cool completely. Serve either black over ice or with your milk of choice.

Brew time: 20–30 minutes

Brewing process: Brewed hot, then cooled over ice

Served: Diluted with milk, often with sugar or flavoured syrups, over ice

Flavour: Weaker than cold brew, due to melting ice, but more bitter

Storage: Drink within 24 hours

Espresso Tonic An easy-to-make, bubbly and refreshing alternative to iced coffee.

MAKES 1 GLASS

- 1 shot espresso, cooled
- ice
- tonic water, chilled
- lime wedge, to serve

Brew a shot of espresso and let it cool. Add some ice to a glass and pour tonic water over the top, then pour in the espresso. Wipe the lime wedge round the rim of the glass, squeeze the juice into the drink and then drop the wedge in.

Variations

• Use lemonade instead of tonic.
• Add a square of dark chocolate to the hot espresso, stir until melted, then cool.

Virgin Cold-Brew Colada A delicious,
cooling virgin colada with a coffee twist.

- 120ml cold-brew coffee
  (see page 46)
- 50ml coconut cream
- 50ml coconut plant-
  based milk
- 25ml coconut syrup
- pineapple juice, to taste
- 1 slice of fresh pineapple,
  chopped, plus extra
  to decorate
- crushed ice, to serve

Blitz all the ingredients in a blender until smooth and creamy. Serve in a tall glass over crushed ice. Decorate the rim of the glass with a slice of pineapple.

Cold-Brew Soda

Sometimes hot milky coffee just doesn't cut it. This soda is cool, sweet and refreshing.

MAKES 1 GLASS

– 30ml sugar syrup
  (see page 60)
– 2 shots cold-brew coffee
  (see page 46)
– ice
– soda water

Add sugar syrup to the cold-brew coffee and stir. Put some ice in a glass and add some soda water, but make sure you leave enough room to pour the coffee mixture over the top.

Minty Lemon Cold-Brew Soda

Muddle some mint leaves at the bottom of the glass, then add the juice of half a lemon and follow the instructions for Cold-Brew Soda.

Italian Sweet Coffee Cream

Add a spoonful to your coffee for an indulgent burst of sweet vanilla flavour – just like in Italy.

MAKES 1 GLASS

– 600ml full-fat milk
– 1 x 397g can of condensed milk
– 1 teaspoon vanilla extract

Gently heat the full-fat and condensed milk in a small pan to combine. Bring to a simmer while stirring, then remove from the heat. Allow the mixture to cool, then add the vanilla and stir. Pour into a sterilised jar or container and store for up to 10 days in the refrigerator.

Coffee and Banana Smoothie Bowl

This energising bowl of sweet and creamy goodness with a coffee kick is the best way to start your day.

SERVES 1

– 1 medium frozen banana
– 1 shot espresso, cooled
– 120ml oat milk
– 1 rounded dessertspoon
  almond or peanut butter
– 1 level dessertspoon
  chocolate protein powder
– 2 level dessertspoons
  porridge oats

Toppings:
– blueberries
– desiccated coconut or
  coconut chips
– maple syrup, to drizzle

Blitz all the main ingredients in a blender until smooth. Pour into a bowl and decorate with toppings.

Mocha and Amaretto Mousse

A delicious and simple dessert, perfect for any coffee and chocolate lover.

SERVES 4

- 75g dark chocolate, chopped
- 1 shot espresso
- 1 measure amaretto liqueur
- 3 medium eggs
- 3 teaspoons sugar

To serve:
- whipped cream
- grated chocolate
- soft amaretti biscuits, crumbled

Melt the chocolate over a bain-marie or in a microwave on low, slowly. Add the espresso and liqueur and stir well. Separate the yolks and egg whites into separate bowls. Whisk the egg whites with the sugar until they form peaks. Whisk the melted chocolate into the egg yolks then gently fold in the egg whites until the mixture is a uniform chocolate colour. Pour into four small glass dishes and chill in the refrigerator for at least 1 hour. Serve decorated with whipped cream, grated chocolate and crumbled biscuits.

Creamy Coffee Panna Cotta

This silky dessert is the perfect way to end dinner – cooling and not too filling.

SERVES 4

- 250ml full-fat milk
- 1 level tablespoon powdered gelatine
- 3 tablespoons caster sugar
- 2 teaspoons instant espresso powder
- 250ml double cream
- Coffee Syrup (see page 61), to serve

Add the milk to a small saucepan, sprinkle the gelatine over the top and leave for 5 minutes until it is wrinkled. Gently warm the milk to dissolve the gelatine, but do not boil. Add the sugar and espresso powder and simmer. Stir well, then take off the heat. Add the cream to the pan and stir well again. Pour into four martini glasses, then leave to set and cool in the refrigerator for about 3 hours. Serve with a drizzle of Coffee Syrup on top.

No-Bake Creamy Coffee Cheesecake

This cheesecake is simple to make and has a light and creamy coffee flavour. It is delicious, impressive and guaranteed to be a dinner-party hit.

SERVES 8

For the base:
- 200g digestive biscuits
- 50g salted butter, melted
- 2 tablespoons strong-brewed coffee

For the filling:
- 400g creamed cheese
- 100g icing sugar
- 2 shots espresso, cooled
- 350g double cream
- 4 tablespoons milk
- 3 teaspoons gelatine powder

You will also need:
- 20-23cm springform cake tin
- grated chocolate, to serve

To make the base, crush the biscuits into crumbs, add the melted butter and coffee, and mix well. Press the mixture into the bottom of a springform tin. Put the tin in the refrigerator to chill while you make the filling.

To make the filling, beat together the creamed cheese, icing sugar and espresso until creamy and smooth. In a separate large bowl, beat the cream until it thickens and forms stiff peaks. Add the milk to a small pan and sprinkle the gelatine over the top. Leave for about 5 minutes until it is wrinkled, then gently warm the milk to dissolve the gelatine. Stir well. Add some of the creamed cheese mixture to the gelatine and stir well again, then fold the gelatine mixture into the rest of the creamed cheese, add the cream and stir well. Spoon the filling onto the cheesecake base and smooth out using a palette knife. Cover and refrigerate for 4-5 hours. The cheesecake must be firm before you attempt to remove it from the tin. Run a knife round the edge before releasing it from the tin. Serve sprinkled with grated chocolate.

Tiramisu Pots
These individual desserts are easier to make than the classic version and are equally delicious.

– 1 egg yolk
– 2 dessertspoons caster sugar
– 1 teaspoon vanilla extract
– 200ml double cream
– 25g mascarpone
– 12 sponge fingers
– grated dark chocolate, to serve

For the syrup:
– 200ml espresso, cooled
– 2 tablespoons dark coffee liqueur

To make the sweet cream, whisk together the egg yolk, sugar and vanilla in a bowl. Add the cream and mascarpone and whisk well until creamy and forming peaks.

To make the coffee syrup, add the espresso and liqueur to a bowl and stir.

Make one dessert at a time. Allow three sponge fingers per dessert. Break each finger into three pieces and dip into the coffee mixture, then place the three pieces at the bottom of a small glass and put a large dessertspoonful of the cream on top. Repeat twice more to create three layers of cream and sponge. Finish each dessert with a drizzle of the coffee mixture and some grated chocolate. Once you have made all the desserts, transfer them to the refrigerator until just before serving.

Flavoured Syrups These syrups are a good way to add different flavours to drinks and desserts.

Simple Sugar Syrup

This can be used to sweeten cocktails or coffees.
It's a good basic recipe that is easy to add flavours to.
Simply add 700g of caster sugar to a small pan, then
add 100ml of cold water and heat gently to dissolve
the sugar. Cool and pour into a sterilised jar or bottle.
It can be stored in the refrigerator for up to a month.
Makes 100ml of syrup.

Vanilla: Add 1 teaspoon of vanilla extract with the
scrapings of 1 vanilla bean pod to cooled Simple
Sugar Syrup. Sieve before using.

Cinnamon: Add two cinnamon sticks to cooled
Simple Sugar Syrup and allow to steep for 6 hours.
Sieve before using.

Ginger: Add 2.5cm of peeled and sliced ginger to
cooled Simple Sugar Syrup and allow to steep for
a couple of hours. Sieve before using.

Coffee Syrup
This thin syrup is easy to make and delicious in milkshakes and cocktails.

SERVES 4

— 250g brown sugar
— 250ml strong-brewed coffee
— 1 teaspoon vanilla extract

Add the sugar and coffee to a pan and stir over a gentle heat until all the sugar has dissolved. Remove from the heat and stir in the vanilla. Cool completely and sieve into a sterilised container. Store in the refrigerator for up to four weeks.

Sweet

Here are sweet treats galore, made even more delicious with plenty of coffee to flavour them – truffles to give as presents or secretly steal from the fridge, cakes that can be made in minutes when you need a sugar hit and impressive desserts that are easy to make.

Mocha Truffles
Chocolatey with a hint of coffee. Serve with a pot of fresh coffee for maximum pleasure.

MAKES ABOUT 20

- 150ml double cream
- 250g mix of dark and milk chocolate, finely chopped
- 25g butter, cubed
- 1 tablespoon instant espresso powder
- boiling water
- 1 tablespoon dark coffee liqueur
- icing sugar or cocoa powder, to coat

Heat the cream to boiling point in a small pan. Remove from the heat, add the chocolate and butter, and stir until melted and well mixed. Make the espresso powder into a paste with boiling water. Transfer the chocolate mixture to a bowl, add the espresso paste and liqueur and stir until smooth. Then cool in the refrigerator for a couple of hours or overnight, until the mixture is firm.

Add some icing sugar or cocoa powder to a wide bowl. Use a teaspoon to scoop out walnut-size amounts of the mixture, roll into balls and cover in the icing sugar or cocoa powder. It is important to have cool hands and to work quickly. Once you have made all the truffles, store them in the refrigerator until serving, as they will soften at room temperature. They can be kept in the refrigerator for up to a week.

Coffee Creams
Another winning coffee and chocolate combination. These delicious treats will melt in your mouth.

MAKES ABOUT 30

- 1 egg white
- 350g icing sugar, sieved
- 2 heaped teaspoons instant espresso powder
- 50g dark chocolate, melted, for drizzling or dipping

You will also need:
- baking tray
- nonstick baking paper

Whisk the egg white until it is bubbly and frothy. Gently mix the icing sugar and coffee powder together with a fork. Add the egg white to the icing sugar mixture, a little at a time, to make a firm dough. Knead well, using your hands. Place your dough on a chopping board that has been dusted with icing sugar and roll it out until it is about 0.5cm thick. Using a small, coin-sized cutter, cut out 30 sweets. Transfer the sweets onto a baking tray lined with baking paper and allow them to harden overnight in the refrigerator. Once hard, use a fork or teaspoon to drizzle melted chocolate back and forth over the sweets, then return them to the refrigerator to set for an hour before serving.

Golden Toffee Popcorn

Fill cellophane bags with this popcorn and tie with ribbon for a great gift.

MAKES 1
MEDIUM BOWL

- 125g Plain Popcorn
  (see below)
- 2 shots espresso
- 125g caster sugar
- 60ml golden syrup
- ½ tablespoon butter
- ½ teaspoon instant
  espresso powder

Place the popcorn in a large mixing bowl. Add the espresso, sugar, golden syrup and butter to a pan and gently heat. Stir until the butter has melted and everything is well mixed. Add the espresso powder and stir again. Drizzle the coffee mixture over the popcorn and stir. Allow the popcorn to cool, then break it up and store in an airtight container.

Plain Popcorn

Add 60ml of vegetable oil to a large saucepan over a medium heat. Add 125g of popcorn kernels to the pan and swirl to coat in the oil. Wait for the kernels to start popping, gently shaking the pan occasionally. Once the popping has stopped, remove the pan from the heat and allow the popcorn to cool.

Maple and Coffee Nuts A delicious
sweet snack to serve after dinner, with coffee.

MAKES 500G

- 4 tablespoons
  brown sugar
- 2 tablespoons maple syrup
- 3 teaspoons instant
  espresso powder
- 1 teaspoon ground
  Himalayan salt
- 3 tablespoons cold water
- 500g roasted unsalted
  mixed nuts
- 1 teaspoon vanilla extract

You will also need:
- baking tray
- nonstick baking paper

Preheat the oven to 180°C (Gas 4). Place the sugar, syrup, espresso powder and salt in a small saucepan. Add the water and gently heat until simmering and well mixed. Simmer until all the sugar has dissolved, then take off the heat and add the nuts and vanilla. Stir well to coat the nuts, then transfer them to a baking tray lined with baking paper. Spread the syrup-coated nuts out and bake in the oven for approximately 15 minutes – the coating on the nuts should feel slightly tacky. Set aside to cool for 30–40 minutes, then break up and serve.

Cardamom and Coffee Mug Cake

An easy cake that can be made in minutes, perfect for when you fancy something sweet.

MAKES 1 MUG CAKE

– butter, for greasing
– 2 tablespoons self-raising flour
– 2 dessertspoons brown sugar
– 1 medium egg
– 2 teaspoons olive oil
– ½ teaspoon vanilla extract
– ½ teaspoon cardamom powder
– 1 level teaspoon instant espresso powder

Butter the inside of a large mug. Add all the ingredients to the mug and mix well with a fork - try to get rid of as many lumps as possible. Microwave on high for 1 minute, or until risen and sponge-like. Let cool for 1 minute, then tuck in. Best eaten warm.

Cinnamon and Coffee Toast This recipe makes an easy weekend breakfast or late-night snack.

- 2 eggs, beaten
- 50ml full-fat milk
- 1 shot espresso, cooled
- 1 tablespoon maple syrup
- 1 teaspoon vanilla extract
- ½ teaspoon ground cinnamon
- 4 medium slices white bread
- butter, for frying
- maple syrup and crispy bacon, to serve

Whisk the eggs, milk, espresso, maple syrup, vanilla and cinnamon together in a wide bowl to make a smooth batter. Soak the bread in the batter, a slice at a time. Heat a heavy-based frying pan to a medium heat, then add butter to the pan – a couple of teaspoons for each slice. Melt the butter and fry each slice for about 2–3 minutes on each side, until golden brown and crisp. Cut the toast in half and serve drizzled with maple syrup and crispy bacon.

Chocolate and Coffee Fridge Cake

Fridge cakes are easy to make, and this one is perfect for a late-afternoon sugar and caffeine hit!

MAKES 16 SQUARES

- 200g milk chocolate, chopped
- 100g butter
- 150ml golden syrup
- 1 dessertspoon instant espresso powder
- 200g digestive biscuits, crushed
- icing sugar, for dusting

You will also need:
- 20cm square brownie tin
- heatproof cling film

Line a 20cm square brownie tin with cling film. Gently melt the chocolate, butter and golden syrup in a saucepan over a low heat. Add the espresso powder and stir well, then add the crushed biscuits and stir again. Spoon the mixture into the brownie tin and smooth out. Chill in the refrigerator for a couple of hours, or until hardened. Cut into 16 squares, dust with icing sugar and serve with a cup of coffee.

Roasted Pears A simple but impressive
dessert to serve at a dinner party.

SERVES 4

- 4 large, ripe pears
- golden caster sugar, for sprinkling
- 25g butter, melted, for drizzling
- Glossy Coffee Sauce (see below) and vanilla ice cream, to serve

Preheat the oven to 180°C (Gas 4). Peel, core and halve your pears and place them face down in a lightly oiled roasting tin. Lightly sprinkle with the sugar then drizzle with the butter. Cook in the oven for approximately 40 minutes, or until soft and golden. Drizzle with Glossy Coffee Sauce and serve with vanilla ice cream.

Glossy Coffee Sauce Perfect over roasted
pears and vanilla ice cream.

- 175g golden caster sugar
- 25g butter
- 3 shots espresso
- 175ml water
- 50ml whipping cream
- 1 small pinch of salt

Gently heat the sugar and butter in a pan with the espresso and water until it all melts. Stir well, then bring to a boil. Reduce the heat and simmer until the sauce reduces to become thick and glossy. Remove the pan from the heat and whisk in the whipping cream and a pinch of salt. The sauce should look glossy and have a sticky texture. If it is too runny, return to the heat and boil for a couple more minutes. Serve with Roasted Pears (see above).

Japanese Coffee Jelly
An elegant dessert that looks as good as it tastes.

SERVES 4

– 3 teaspoons
  gelatine powder
– 4 shots espresso
– 75g brown sugar
– 180ml boiling water
– 240ml cold water
– double cream, to serve

Put the gelatine, espresso and sugar into a large jug and pour the boiling water over the ingredients. Whisk well until the gelatine and sugar have dissolved. Add the cold water and whisk well again. Pour the jelly into martini glasses and place in the refrigerator for approximately 3 hours, or until set. Serve with double cream poured on top to make a creamy layer.

Mocha Tart A deliciously rich tart, perfect
for special occasions.

SERVES 8

– 225g ready-made
  shortcrust pastry, chilled
– 300ml double cream
– 1 tablespoon golden
  caster sugar
– 1 tablespoon instant
  espresso powder
– 200g dark chocolate,
  chopped
– 50g salted butter
– cream or ice cream,
  to serve

You will also need:
– 18cm round tart tin
– heatproof cling film
– ceramic baking beans

Preheat the oven to 190°C (Gas 5). Roll out
the pastry, enough for an 18cm round tart tin.
Line the tin with the pastry, then trim off any
overhanging pastry. Top the pastry with heatproof
cling film and add ceramic baking beans. Cook
the pastry case for 20 minutes, remove the beans
and film, and cook for a further 5 minutes. Set
the case aside to cool.

Gently warm the cream, sugar, espresso powder,
chocolate and butter over a low heat until melted
and stir well. Take the mixture off the heat. Stir,
then leave to cool for 10 minutes before pouring
into the pastry case. Do not fill the case to the
top. Cool the tart in the refrigerator for a couple
of hours, or until set, before serving. Serve with
cream or ice cream.

Espresso Risotto with Roasted Oranges
Coffee and orange flavours give this dish an unexpected twist.

SERVES 4

– 450ml full-fat milk
– 2 tablespoons sugar
– 100g risotto rice
– 2 tablespoons dark coffee liqueur
– 2 shots espresso
– roasted oranges, to serve

For the roasted oranges:
– 2 oranges
– olive oil
– sugar
– ground cinnamon

You will also need:
– baking tray
– aluminium foil

Warm the milk and sugar in a large pan on the hob. Once simmering, add the rice and stir. Cook the risotto gently for 20-25 minutes, or until the rice has softened but retains bite. Add a little more milk if the rice becomes too dry. Stir in the liqueur and coffee and mix well. Gently cook for another 5-10 minutes or until you have your desired consistency. Serve in coffee cups with roasted oranges on the side.

Roasted oranges
Preheat the oven to 180°C (Gas 4). Line a baking tray with aluminium foil. Slice two oranges into rounds. Place the rounds on the baking tray, drizzle with a little olive oil and sprinkle with a little sugar and ground cinnamon. Bake in the oven for about 15-20 minutes. Serve with the Espresso Risotto, allowing approximately half an orange per person.

WHAT TO DO WITH LEFTOVER COFFEE GROUNDS

If you're regularly making coffee at home, you're going to find yourself with a lot of leftover grounds. Rather than just throwing them away, try these ideas.

FERTILISE YOUR GARDEN

Coffee grounds contain nitrogen, calcium, potassium, iron, phosphorus, magnesium and chromium, all of which will help fertilise your soil, nourish your plants and attract worms. Simply sprinkle cooled leftover grounds onto your soil.

ADD TO COMPOST

Compost made with plant food waste and coffee grounds is nutrient rich and very good for the garden. Adding coffee grounds to compost also helps to decrease greenhouse gas emissions.

MAKE A BODY OR LIP SCRUB

Coarse coffee grounds are good for exfoliation. Melt a small amount of coconut oil in a bowl in the microwave. Add a couple of spoonfuls of grounds and mix well. Rub into your hands and body to help remove dead skin cells, then rinse off in the shower. To make a lip scrub, add honey to some grounds and use on your lips.

MAKE A NATURAL DYE

If you are making a costume and want to age an old white T-shirt, simply add a bit of water to some coffee grounds to create a natural dye that works on paper, cotton and linen.

TENDERISE MEAT

The acidity in coffee helps to keep meat soft and tender, and also enhances flavour. Add coffee grounds to your steak with salt and oil for tasty flavour and a crisp crust.

TREAT SCRATCHES ON FURNITURE

Before purchasing a commercial treatment, try using some coffee grounds on your scratched furniture. Make a thick paste by adding water to the grounds. Rub the mixture into the scratch and leave it for 5-10 minutes, then remove with a clean cloth. Repeat this process until you get the required colour match - you might have to leave the coffee on for longer if you need to achieve a strong colour.

Baked

The joys of baking are well known – the relaxing stirring, the delicious aromas that pervade the kitchen and that first taste of a warm cookie, fresh from the oven. There is nothing not to like about making cakes, biscuits and bread, and these bakes made with coffee are perfect for breakfast, lunch and dinner.

Chocolate and Coffee Cookies Golden, crisp and chewy, and perfect to serve with coffee.

MAKES 16 COOKIES

- 125g salted butter
- 125g caster sugar
- ½ teaspoon baking powder
- 150g plain flour
- 1 large egg, beaten
- 1 level tablespoon instant espresso powder, mixed with a little water to make a paste
- 150g milk or dark chocolate, finely chopped

You will also need:
- baking tray
- nonstick baking paper

Preheat the oven to 180°C (Gas 4). Cream the butter and sugar together until light and fluffy. Add baking powder to the flour and gently mix. Add a little of the egg to the butter mixture, alternating with a little of the flour, stirring in between each addition, until all used up. Add the espresso paste and stir, then add the chocolate and gently fold in.

Line a baking tray with baking paper. Spoon 8 dessertspoons of the mixture onto the tray, leaving room in between each spoonful as the cookies will spread. Bake in the preheated oven for about 12 minutes, or until golden, crispy around the edge and soft in the middle. Remove the cookies to cool and bake the second batch.

Coffee Kisses

These biscuits, sandwiched together with Coffee Buttercream, are an excellent addition to a morning or afternoon cup of coffee.

MAKES 12

- 2½ teaspoons instant espresso powder
- 1 teaspoon boiling water
- 150g self-raising flour
- 75g caster sugar
- 75g unsalted butter, cubed
- 1 medium egg, beaten
- Coffee Buttercream (see page 85), for sandwiching

You will also need:
- baking tray
- nonstick baking paper

Preheat the oven to 180°C (Gas 4). Add the espresso powder to a cup, then add the boiling water, mix to a paste and set aside to cool. Add the flour and sugar to a large mixing bowl and gently mix. Add the butter to the flour mixture and rub in using your fingertips until you have a coarse crumb-like texture. Add the beaten egg to the cooled coffee and gently beat using a fork. Add the coffee mixture to the crumb mixture and work in using a fork, then use your hands to make a soft dough. Knead the dough well.

Line a large baking tray with baking paper, then, using your hands, roll the dough into 24 walnut-size balls. Place half of them onto the baking tray and flatten, leaving space between each for spreading. You will need to make two batches of 12 biscuits. Bake each batch in the oven for about 15 minutes, or until golden. Allow the biscuits to cool, then sandwich them together with the Coffee Buttercream to make perfect kisses.

Coffee Buttercream

This recipe makes enough buttercream to sandwich together a cake and ice the top, or to sandwich together a full batch of Coffee Kisses (see page 84).

- 1 rounded teaspoon instant espresso powder
- 1 teaspoon boiling water
- 100g unsalted butter, softened
- 200g icing sugar, sieved

Add the espresso powder to a cup, then add the boiling water, mix to a paste and set aside to cool. Beat the butter and icing sugar together until soft and fluffy. Add the cooled coffee mixture and beat well together.

Simple Biscotti

These easy-to-make Italian treats originated in Tuscany in the 14th century. The word *biscotti* means 'twice baked'. While biscotti don't contain coffee, they are the perfect shape and crunchiness for serving with and dipping in coffee.

MAKES 25

- 150g shelled almonds
- 2 medium eggs
- 150g golden caster sugar
- zest of 1 lemon
- 300g plain flour
- 1 teaspoon baking powder

You will also need:
- baking tray
- nonstick baking paper

Preheat the oven to 200°C (Gas 6). Roast the almonds on a baking tray for about 5 minutes and then chop them roughly. Beat the eggs and the sugar together well, until pale in colour and increased in size. Add the nuts and the zest, then sieve in the flour and baking powder. Mix well, then use your hands to form a dough. Divide the dough into two, then roll each half out on a floured surface using your hands, to make two long log shapes about 4cm wide and 25cm long.

Place the logs on a lined baking tray and bake for 20 minutes, or until just golden. Reduce the oven to 150°C (Gas 2). Let the logs cool for a few minutes, then slice them into long pieces 1cm wide using a sharp bread knife. Lay them back on the baking tray and return to the oven for another 15–20 minutes, to dry out. They should be crispy, crunchy and golden. Serve them with coffee, always.

Honey-Drizzled Espresso Cakes

These cupcakes are sticky, sweet and delicious with a light coffee and honey flavour.

MAKES 12

- 150g salted butter, softened
- 150g muscovado sugar
- 175g self-raising flour
- 3 large eggs, beaten
- boiling water
- 3 teaspoons instant espresso powder

For the honey drizzle:
- 4 teaspoons honey
- 50g icing sugar, sieved
- 1-2 teaspoons water

You will also need:
- 12-hole cupcake tray
- paper cupcake cases

Preheat the oven to 180°C (Gas 4) and line a cupcake tray with paper cases. Cream the butter and sugar in a mixing bowl until light and fluffy. Add the flour and eggs alternately, a little of each at a time, stirring well. Add a splash of boiling water to the coffee powder and mix, then add the coffee to the cake batter and stir in well. Add a dessertspoon of the cake batter to each of the paper cases and bake for 20 minutes in the preheated oven. Allow the cakes to cool.

To make the drizzle, add the honey to the icing sugar and add the water a teaspoon at a time, mixing well until thick but runny. Drizzle back and forth over the top of the cooled cakes using a teaspoon. Let the drizzle set before serving. Alternatively, top the cakes with Coffee Buttercream (see page 85), if preferred.

Marbled Mocha Loaf with Vanilla Glaze
A blend of coffee, chocolate and vanilla gives this cake an unbeatable flavour and an impressive appearance.

MAKES 1 SMALL LOAF

- 125g salted butter
- 125g caster sugar
- 1 teaspoon baking powder
- 125g self-raising flour
- 2 eggs, beaten
- 1 teaspoon vanilla extract
- 1 teaspoon instant
  espresso powder
- 1 teaspoon cocoa powder
- splash of boiling water
- butter, for greasing
- Vanilla Glaze (see page 91)

You will also need:
- loaf tin
- nonstick baking paper

Preheat the oven to 180°C (Gas 4). Cream the butter and sugar together until light and fluffy. Add the baking powder to the flour and stir. Add a little of the egg and stir, then add a little sieved flour and mix. Repeat, alternating, until all the egg and flour are used up. Stir the batter well, then divide evenly into two separate bowls.

Add the vanilla to one bowl and stir. Mix the espresso powder and cocoa powder together and add a splash of boiling water to make a smooth paste. Add the paste to the other bowl and stir. Grease and line a loaf tin with baking paper. To get a marbled effect, spoon the two batters into the tin to create a chequered pattern. Build up layers by placing the mocha batter on top of the vanilla and vice versa. Gently run a fork through the batters to create a marbled pattern.

Bake in the preheated oven for about 45 minutes, or until the top is springy to touch and an inserted knife or toothpick comes out clean. Transfer the cake to a wire rack to cool. Once cooled, drizzle the top of the cake with Vanilla Glaze. Let the glaze set before serving.

Vanilla Glaze
This glaze works well on biscuits and doughnuts as well as cakes. Drizzle it back and forth using a teaspoon or fork.

- 150g icing sugar
- 3 tablespoons semi-skimmed milk, plus extra if needed
- 2 teaspoons vanilla extract

Sieve the icing sugar into a bowl and add the milk and vanilla, a little at a time. Stir well until you have a pourable glaze. If the mixture is too stiff, add extra milk a teaspoon at a time until you achieve the right consistency.

Mocha Brownies with Salted Caramel Sauce Rich and fudgy, with a smooth and salty topping.

MAKES 16

- 200g dark chocolate, chopped
- 175g butter
- 2 tablespoons instant espresso powder
- 3 medium eggs
- 200g golden caster sugar
- 1 teaspoon vanilla extract
- 1 tablespoon maple syrup
- 100g self-raising flour
- 200g milk chocolate, chopped
- Salted Caramel Sauce (see page 93), to serve

You will also need:
- 23cm square brownie tin
- nonstick baking paper

Preheat the oven to 180°C (Gas 4). Grease and line a brownie tin with baking paper. Melt the dark chocolate and butter in a heatproof bowl in the microwave, 10 seconds at a time, then stir to mix in the coffee. In a separate bowl, beat the eggs and sugar together, then add the chocolate mixture, vanilla and maple syrup. Sieve in the flour and stir until thick and glossy. Fold the chopped milk chocolate into the mixture and pour into the lined tin. Use a spatula to spread the mixture out, then bake in the oven for approximately 30 minutes, or until crispy on the outside and soft and fudgy in the middle. Plunge the bottom of the tin into cold water to stop the cooking, taking care not to get the brownies wet, then cool fully in the tin. Cut into 16 squares and serve with Salted Caramel Sauce.

Salted Caramel Sauce

Delicious on all desserts and ice cream, but especially good on brownies. Also perfect eaten cold for a late-night snack!

MAKES ENOUGH FOR
16 BROWNIES

– 175g brown sugar
– 300ml double cream
– 50g salted butter
– ½ teaspoon salt

Add all the ingredients to a small pan and gently warm on the hob, stirring continuously until the sugar has dissolved. Turn up the heat so that the sauce bubbles and becomes golden and glossy. Stir well, then remove from the heat and allow to cool before serving. Serve with Mocha Brownies (see page 92).

Coffee and Date Traybake

This sweet treat is rich and full of flavour. Using ready-rolled pastry makes it quick and easy to prepare, ready to enjoy with a mid-morning or after-dinner coffee.

MAKES 16 SLICES

- 250g pitted dates, chopped
- 75ml espresso
- zest of half an orange
- 2 sheets ready-rolled sweetcrust pastry
- butter, for greasing
- milk, for glazing
- caster sugar, for sprinkling

You will also need:

- 20cm square brownie tin
- nonstick baking paper

Preheat the oven to 200°C (Gas 6). Place the dates, espresso and orange zest in a saucepan on the hob and gently warm for about 4-5 minutes or until the mixture is soft and sticky. Set aside to cool. Butter a brownie tin and line with baking paper. Cut one of the sheets of pastry so that it fits the base and gently press it into the corners. Spread the cooled date mixture over the pastry then top with the second pastry sheet that has been cut to size. Gently push the pastry down and into the corners. Bake in the oven for 25-30 minutes, or until golden brown. Allow to cool in the tin then cut into approximately 16 slices.

MATCHING FLAVOURS WITH COFFEE

Coffee obviously goes well with milk, sugar and chocolate, but there are so many other flavours that make a perfect pairing with coffee, either as an addition to a drink or to complement a cup of coffee. Coffee has many notes that make it a great match for a range of different flavours:

- Almond
- Banana
- Beef
- Berries
- Blackcurrant
- Caramel
- Cardamom
- Chai
- Cheese
- Chocolate
- Cinnamon
- Coconut
- Ginger
- Hazelnut
- Mint
- Nutmeg
- Orange
- Pumpkin
- Rose
- Vanilla
- Walnut

Cappuccino Cake with Creamy Frosting

A modern update on traditional coffee cake. All walnuts have been banished, replaced by creamy frosting topped with grated chocolate.

SERVES 8-10

- 200g self-raising flour
- 1 teaspoon baking powder
- 2 teaspoons instant espresso powder
- 200g unsalted butter, softened
- 100g caster sugar
- 100g light brown sugar
- 4 medium eggs, beaten
- boiling water
- Creamy Vanilla Frosting (see below), for sandwiching and topping
- grated milk chocolate, to decorate

You will also need:
- 2 x 23cm springform cake tins

Preheat the oven to 180°C (Gas 4). Gently mix the flour, baking powder and espresso powder together. Beat the butter with the sugars until soft, light and fluffy. Add a little of the egg and stir, then a little sieved flour and mix. Repeat, alternating, until all the egg and flour are used up. For a smooth and glossy cake batter, add a splash of boiling water and stir well. Divide the batter between two well-greased springform cake tins. Bake in the oven for approximately 20 minutes or until golden and an inserted knife or toothpick comes out clean. Remove the cakes from the tins and allow them to cool. Sandwich the cakes together with the frosting and spread the remaining frosting onto the top of the cake using a palette knife. Top with grated chocolate.

Creamy Vanilla Frosting

Place 250g of sieved icing sugar, 80g of softened unsalted butter, 25ml of whole milk and ½ a teaspoon of vanilla extract in a bowl and beat until light, fluffy and creamy. This will be enough to sandwich a cake together and cover the top.

Coffee and Banana Cake

This alternative to classic banana bread is boosted by coffee and sweet sultanas. It's an excellent way to use up any ripe bananas in the fruit bowl.

SERVES 8-10

- 75g sultanas
- 2 measures dark coffee liqueur
- 175g self-raising flour
- 2 teaspoons instant espresso powder
- 125g salted butter, melted, plus extra for greasing
- ½ tablespoon golden caster sugar
- 2 large eggs, beaten
- 3 medium ripe bananas, mashed

You will also need:
- small loaf tin
- nonstick baking paper

Preheat the oven to 180°C (Gas 4). Place the sultanas in a small bowl and pour the coffee liqueur over them, and leave them to steep while you prepare the cake batter. Place the flour and espresso powder in a large mixing bowl and stir to combine. In another large mixing bowl, mix the melted butter and sugar until blended, then add the beaten eggs and the mashed bananas and stir well together. Drain the sultanas and add them to the butter mixture with a couple of teaspoons of the leftover liqueur. Add the flour a tablespoon at a time and mix well to get a lumpy, speckled batter. Grease a loaf tin and line it with baking paper. Spoon the batter into the tin and bake for about 1 hour, or until golden and an inserted knife or toothpick comes out clean – the top of the cake should bounce back when pressed. Eat warm from the oven or set aside to cool and store in an airtight container.

Coffee Soda Bread
This lovely dense bread is best eaten warm with butter.

MAKES 1 LOAF

- 300g plain white flour, plus extra for sprinkling
- 1 teaspoon baking powder
- 2 tablespoons instant espresso powder
- 75g caster sugar
- 300ml buttermilk

Preheat the oven to 180°C (Gas 4). Mix the flour, baking powder, espresso powder and sugar in a bowl, then add the buttermilk. Using your hands, bring it all together into a dough. Turn the dough out onto a floured surface, knead for about 1 minute then shape into a ball. Flatten the ball a little then cut a deep cross into the top. Sprinkle the top with a little flour then bake in the oven for about 40 minutes, or until the bottom of the loaf sounds hollow when tapped.

Coffee Butter
Serve this delicious butter on toast, bread or pancakes.

- ½ teaspoon boiled water
- 1 teaspoon instant espresso powder
- 50g salted butter, softened
- 1 dessertspoon icing sugar

Make a paste by adding the boiled water to the espresso powder. Beat the butter, icing sugar and espresso paste together with a spoon until smooth. Serve immediately or store in the refrigerator.

Coffee Scones
Eat these warm from the oven with butter – or Coffee Butter for extra flavour.

MAKES 15

- 300g plain flour, sieved
- 125g caster sugar
- 2 teaspoons
  baking powder
- ½ teaspoon salt
- 100g chilled salted
  butter, cubed
- 50ml strong-brewed coffee
- 2 teaspoons instant
  espresso powder
- 1 teaspoon vanilla extract
- 120ml buttermilk
- 1 large egg, beaten
- butter or Coffee Butter
  (see page 100), to serve

You will also need:
- 6cm round cutter
- baking tray
- nonstick baking paper

Preheat the oven to 200°C (Gas 6). Gently mix the flour, sugar, baking powder and salt in a large bowl. Add the butter to the flour mix and rub in using your fingertips until you have a fine, crumb-like texture. In a separate bowl, mix the coffee, espresso powder and vanilla. Allow to cool, then add the buttermilk and the egg and mix well.

Make a well in your crumb mixture and add the coffee mixture, then gently stir until you have a crumbly dough. The dough will be quite sticky, so ensure you have a well-floured surface to knead on – add extra flour if necessary. Gently knead the dough, then roll out on the floured surface until the dough is about 1.5–2cm thick. Using a 6cm round cutter, cut out your scones and chill in the refrigerator for 20 minutes on a lined baking tray; leave room between each scone as they will spread. Brush a little milk onto the top of the scones, then bake in the oven for 20 minutes, or until golden brown and cooked through. Serve with butter or Coffee Butter.

Iced

Unleash the blender, empty the freezer and rejoice at these ice-laden drinks, lollies and desserts – perfect for summer parties, post-workout treats or enjoying by the pool. Easy to make, iced to perfection and just what you need on hot days.

Coconut Frappé Tropical and refreshing – a perfect summer drink.

- 300ml plant-based
  coconut milk
- 2 tablespoons
  coconut syrup
- 1 dessertspoon instant
  espresso powder
- 4 ice cubes
- whipped cream, to serve
- grated chocolate, to serve

Blitz the coconut milk, coconut syrup and espresso powder in a blender on low until mixed. Add the ice cubes one by one, and blitz again until frothy. Serve topped with whipped cream and grated chocolate.

Croatian Iced Coffee So much more
than just coffee on ice!

– 2 shots espresso
– 2 dessertspoons Chocolate
  Syrup (see below)
– 2 scoops vanilla ice cream
– 300ml milk
– 4 ice cubes
– whipped cream, to serve
– grated chocolate, to serve

Blitz the espresso, syrup, ice cream and milk in
a blender on low until mixed. Add the ice cubes
one by one, and blitz again. Serve topped with
whipped cream and grated chocolate.

Chocolate Syrup An excellent addition
to coffee drinks and desserts.

– 50g caster sugar
– 300ml water
– 125g dark chocolate,
  chopped

Heat the sugar and water gently in a pan until
dissolved. Boil for 1 minute, then take the
pan off the heat and stir in the chocolate until
melted. Reheat to make a shiny syrup.

Ice Cubes for Coffee

The joy of drinking iced coffee is diminished when the ice melts and dilutes the drink. These ice cubes are easy to make and store and will ensure that you have a delicious drink right to the last sip.

Brewed coffee ice cubes

Brew coffee using your chosen method (see page 20). Allow it to cool to room temperature then pour into a silicone ice-cube tray. Freeze for 3–4 hours, then transfer the cubes to a freezer bag and store in the freezer.

Mocha ice cubes

Make 150ml of cold-brew coffee (see page 46), then mix with 1 dessertspoon of Chocolate Syrup (see page 105) and 250ml of milk or oat milk. Pour into a silicone ice-cube tray. Freeze overnight, then transfer the cubes to a freezer bag and store in the freezer. These ice cubes are delicious in iced or cold-brew coffee and milkshakes.

Maple coffee ice cubes

Brew coffee using your chosen method (see page 20) and sweeten to taste with maple syrup. Stir well, then allow to cool to room temperature and pour into a silicone ice-cube tray. Freeze for 3–4 hours, then transfer the cubes to a freezer bag and store in the freezer.

Vanilla ice cubes

Place 250ml of milk or oat milk, 150ml of condensed milk, 2 teaspoons of golden caster sugar and 1½ teaspoons of vanilla essence in a milk pan on the hob. Warm gently to mix and dissolve the sugar, then allow to cool to room temperature and pour into a silicone ice-cube tray. Freeze overnight, then transfer the cubes to a freezer bag and store in the freezer. Delicious in iced or cold-brew coffee.

Caramel ice cubes

Place 250ml of almond milk, 150ml of condensed milk, 2 teaspoons of brown sugar and 2 teaspoons of caramel syrup in a milk pan on the hob. Warm gently to mix and dissolve the sugar, then allow to cool to room temperature and pour into a silicone ice-cube tray. Freeze overnight, then transfer the cubes to a freezer bag and store in the freezer. Delicious in iced or cold-brew coffee.

Minty ice cubes

Place a handful of chopped mint leaves with 2 teaspoons of vanilla essence and 1 dessertspoon of caster sugar in a jug. Add 300ml of slightly cooled boiled water and stir to dissolve the sugar. Allow the mixture to cool to room temperature then sieve and pour into a silicone ice-cube tray. Freeze for 3-4 hours, then transfer the cubes to a freezer bag and store in the freezer. Perfect in cold-brew coffee.

Coffee Granita An impressive dinner-party
dessert that is easy to make in advance.

SERVES 6

- 500ml strong-brewed
  coffee, hot
- 5g brown sugar
- 100ml dark coffee liqueur
- single cream, to serve
- grated chocolate, to serve

In a large jug, mix the hot coffee and sugar, stirring well until dissolved. Allow the coffee to cool, then add the liqueur. Once fully cooled, add the mixture to a shallow ice-cream container and freeze for 1 hour, or until starting to become slushy. Use a fork to mix up the ice crystals then freeze for a further 20–30 minutes, repeating the process until you have the desired texture. Serve in glass bowls with a splash of cream and some grated chocolate.

Espresso Slush Simple and refreshing,
this drink can be served with a slice of lemon.

MAKES 1 DRINK

- 2 shots espresso,
  sweetened to taste
  and cooled
- 5–6 ice cubes
- slice of lemon, to serve

Put the espresso in a blender and add the ice cubes one at a time, blitzing after each until you have a slushy texture. Pour into a glass and serve with a slice of lemon.

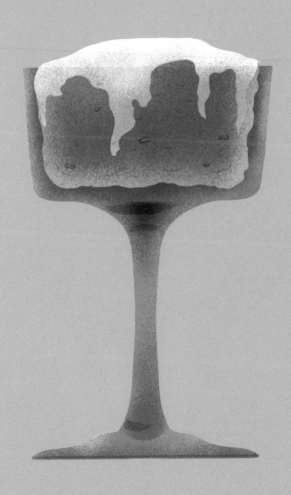

Affogato

The Italian word *affogato* means 'drowned' in English. Drown a scoop of vanilla gelato in a shot of espresso for a creamy, sharp and sweet dessert. It's the perfect ending to a meal – especially if you can't decide whether you want dessert or coffee!

Variations

- Add some crumbled amaretti biscuits or biscotti to the ice cream.
- Add a splash of liqueur to the coffee – try grappa, Drambuie or brandy.

Coffee Ice Cream

An easy, make-at-home version of a favourite dessert.

MAKES ABOUT 600ML

- 1 x 397g can condensed milk
- 150ml strong-brewed coffee
- 300ml double cream
- melted chocolate, for drizzling

Mix the condensed milk with the coffee and chill in the refrigerator. Whip the double cream until thick then fold into the chilled coffee. Freeze in a sealed ice-cream container for about 6 hours. Give it a really good stir after a couple of hours to break up the ice crystals, then return to the freezer. Serve the ice cream drizzled with melted chocolate.

Minty Coffee Lollies
Mint adds a refreshing twist to this creamy frozen coffee treat.

MAKES 6

- 1 large handful chopped mint leaves
- 450ml strong-brewed coffee
- 120ml condensed milk

You will also need:
- lolly moulds

Place the mint leaves in a heatproof bowl and pour the hot coffee over them. Stir well and allow to steep for approximately 30–60 minutes. Strain the coffee into a jug and add the condensed milk. Stir well to combine, then pour into lolly moulds, leaving room at the top for the lollies to expand. Freeze for about 6 hours, or until fully frozen. Remove the lollies from the moulds and serve immediately.

Coffee and Caramel Lollies

Serve as a sweet, rich and decadent dessert.

MAKES 8

- 450ml strong-
  brewed coffee
- 120ml oat milk
- 50ml caramel syrup
- 1 level tablespoon
  brown sugar

You will also need:
- lolly moulds

Place all the ingredients in a small saucepan and gently warm to dissolve the sugar. Stir well, then allow the mixture to cool. Pour into lolly moulds, leaving room at the top for the lollies to expand. Freeze for about 6 hours, or until fully frozen. Remove the lollies from the moulds and serve immediately.

Coconut and Coffee Lollies

Delicious summer flavours for a hot day.

MAKES 4

- 225ml strong-
  brewed coffee
- 120ml plant-based
  coconut milk
- ½ tablespoon brown sugar
- melted chocolate, cooled,
  to drizzle

You will also need:
- lolly moulds

In a large jug, mix the coffee, milk and sugar, stirring until the sugar has dissolved. Allow the mixture to cool. Pour into lolly moulds, leaving room at the top for the lollies to expand. Freeze for about 6 hours, or until fully frozen. Remove the lollies from the moulds and use a fork to drizzle chocolate over them before serving.

Tipsy Orange and Coffee Lollies

Perfect to enjoy when the weather is hot, with a little alcoholic kick that makes them a hit at parties.

MAKES 6

- 450ml strong-
  brewed coffee
- 2 measures orange liqueur
- 1 tablespoon brown sugar
- zest of 1 orange,
  finely grated

You will also need:
- lolly moulds

In a large jug, mix the coffee, orange liqueur, sugar and zest, stirring until the sugar has dissolved. Allow the mixture to cool. Pour into lolly moulds, leaving room at the top for the lollies to expand. Freeze for about 6 hours, or until fully frozen. Remove the lollies from the moulds and serve immediately.

Spicy

Coffee pairs perfectly with sweet things, but it can also be an unusual complement to steaks, ribs, chilli and more. Rub it on and mix it in to take savoury dishes to a whole new level, then see if your family and friends can guess the secret ingredient!

Coffee Steak

Take four room-temperature steaks, drizzle with olive oil, season with plenty of salt and pepper, then sprinkle them with freshly ground coffee, followed by brown sugar. Turn the steaks over and repeat. Cook in a pan on a high heat, or on the barbecue, to create a crust. Cook for about 6 minutes, turning every minute for medium rare. Cook for longer if you like your steak well done. Serve with green vegetables. Serves 4.

Cod with Coffee-Buttered Noodles
A simple, quick and impressive dinner for two.

SERVES 2

For the cod:
- 2 x cod loins
- olive oil spray
- 1 lemon, halved
- cayenne pepper

For the noodles:
- 300g Singapore rice noodles
- 25g salted butter
- 45ml brewed coffee
- 30ml soy sauce
- chopped spring onion and coriander, to garnish
- steamed green beans, to serve

Preheat the oven to 180°C (Gas 4). Place the cod loins on a baking tray lined with aluminium foil, spray with the olive oil, squeeze half a lemon over each loin, then sprinkle with cayenne pepper. Bake the fish in the oven for 20 minutes, or until cooked through.

While the fish is cooking, cook the noodles according to packet instructions and drain. Add the butter, coffee and soy sauce to the hot noodles and gently stir through. Garnish the noodles with the spring onions and coriander and serve with the fish and green beans.

One-Pan Coffee-Roasted Vegetables

Preheat the oven to 180°C (Gas 4). Chop three carrots and three parsnips in half lengthways and lay out in a roasting tin. Mix 2 tablespoons of olive oil with 1 teaspoon of instant coffee powder, ½ a teaspoon of salt and ½ a teaspoon of brown sugar. Pour the oil mixture over the veggies and toss to make sure they are fully covered. Season with salt and pepper and sprinkle with sesame seeds (optional). Roast for about 30 minutes or until soft and browned. Serves 4.

Maple and Coffee Ribs with
BBQ Sauce Coffee adds a counterpoint
to the sweetness of maple syrup.

SERVES 4

- 2 racks of pre-prepared pork ribs
- olive oil, for drizzling
- salt and pepper, to season

For the BBQ sauce:
- 8 tablespoons tomato ketchup
- 4 tablespoons balsamic vinegar
- 4 tablespoons maple syrup
- 1 tablespoon instant espresso powder
- 1 teaspoon paprika
- salt and pepper, to taste

You will also need:
- roasting tin
- aluminium foil

Preheat the oven to 180°C (Gas 4). Drizzle the ribs with olive oil and season with salt and pepper. Place in a roasting tin and cover with foil. Cook for 1 hour, then remove the foil and cook for a further 30 minutes. Warm all the sauce ingredients together in a small pan on the hob. When the sauce comes to a simmer, reduce the heat and whisk to thicken. Serve the ribs drizzled with the sauce.

Crispy Coffee Tofu
This soft-on-the-inside, crispy-on-the-outside tofu soaks up a delicious combination of flavours.

SERVES 4

- 500g firm tofu, drained
- 2 tablespoons dried polenta, for dusting
- salt and pepper, to taste
- sesame oil, for frying

For the sauce:
- 1 shot espresso
- 2 tablespoons light soy sauce
- 2 tablespoons Chinese vinegar
- 2 tablespoons oyster sauce
- 2 tablespoons runny honey

To serve:
- cooked rice
- 2 spring onions, chopped
- handful of coriander leaves, chopped

Preheat the oven on a low heat. Cut the tofu into large strips, dust with the polenta and season with salt and pepper. Heat the sesame oil in a wok and fry the tofu until golden – about 3–5 minutes on each side. Keep the tofu warm in the oven while you make the sauce. Warm all the sauce ingredients together in a pan on the hob. Bring the sauce to a simmer, then turn the heat down low. Serve the tofu with rice, drizzled with the sauce and garnished with spring onions and coriander.

Mocha Chilli A classic chilli recipe, with some
unusual ingredients.

- 1 tablespoon olive oil
- 1 large onion, chopped
- 2 garlic cloves, minced
- 1 small or medium fresh
  red chilli, seeds removed
  and finely chopped
- 500g minced beef
- 2 cans of chopped
  tomatoes
- 1 teaspoon instant
  espresso powder
- 1 tablespoon
  tomato purée
- 25g dark chocolate,
  chopped
- ½ teaspoon sugar
- 1 beef stock cube,
  crumbled
- 1 x 400g can of black
  beans, rinsed
- chilli flakes, to taste
  (optional)
- salt and pepper, to taste

To serve:
- tortillas
- grated cheese
- soured cream
- guacamole

Heat the oil in a large pan. Add the onion, garlic
and chilli and cook until browned slightly and
softened. Add the beef, breaking it up with a
spoon, and continue to cook until the meat is
browned. Add the tomatoes, espresso powder
and tomato purée and cook over a low heat for
about 20 minutes. Add the chocolate, sugar,
stock cube and beans and stir well, then cook for
a further 15 minutes over a low heat. Add a small
sprinkle of chilli flakes, if desired, and season to
taste with salt and pepper. Serve with tortillas,
grated cheese, soured cream and guacamole.

PERFECT COFFEE PAIRINGS

You will have your own favourite things to eat with
a cup of coffee, but if you're looking for inspiration,
here are some delicious suggestions for different
times of day.

BREAKFAST

Scrambled eggs, omelettes, eggs on toast
Crepes and pancakes
Peanut butter and jam on toast
French toast
Banana on toast
Oatmeal with berries and maple syrup
Bacon

MID-MORNING AND
AFTERNOON TEA

Brownies and chocolate cake
Fruit cakes and scones
Panettone
Sweet pastries

LUNCH

Charcuterie
Cheese board
Toasted cheese sandwiches
Smoked salmon and creamed cheese bagel
Cheese on toast
Berry fruit salad

DINNER AND AFTER DINNER

Curry
Steak
Biscotti and amaretti biscuits
Turkish delight
Mint chocolate and salted
caramel chocolate

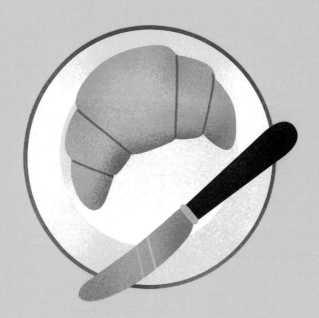

Index

Acknowledgements

With thanks to Dan at Blueprint Coffee and Books, Whitstable, for gifting delicious house-roasted coffee.

About the Author & Illustrator

Sarah Ford has written many giftable bestsellers, including *50 Ways to Kill a Slug*, *What Would Unicorn Do?*, *Be a Flamingo*, *The Chinese Zodiac* and *It's the Little Things*.

Clare Owen is a freelance illustrator and designer currently based in Bristol, UK. Her clients include *Elle* France, *O: The Oprah Magazine,* Chronicle Books, Penguin Random House, Quarto, Hallmark US, Marks and Spencer, and Airbnb.